Become

UNFORGETTABLE

7 STRATEGIES TO SCALE
YOUR PERSONAL BRAND
FOR MAXIMUM IMPACT

Yolanda M. Smith

Become Unforgettable

7 Strategies To Scale Your Personal Brand

For Maximum Impact

Copyright © 2023 by Branding 4 Success

Library of Congress Cataloging-In-Publication Data Branding 4 Success

ISBN 979-8-3907208-9-9

1. Women & Business   2. Image & Etiquette

Library of Congress Control Number:

Book interior and cover design by Abdul Rehman

Printed in the United States of America

First Edition

Contents

Dedication

In memory of my mother Loretta and father Trevor. The indelible footprint you left behind will be the legacy we take forward.

To my children Austin and Madison, my beautiful granddaughter Violet, and my bonus children Victoria and Mase, you are my heartbeats, and the reason I grind like I do. I dare you to dream big, make an impact in this world, and believe you can achieve your heart's desire.

My husband Kenton, thanks for putting up with the long hours and restless nights as I percolate these ideas into something tangible. Your support allowed me to leave my corporate job and pursue my passion. That was a risk you were willing to take.

And my tribe of friends, family and coaches, without the love and support from you, I would cease to be who I am today. You challenge me to step into my purpose and be a better version of myself daily.

I feel the unconditional love from each and every one of you. I appreciate all of you for being who you are, meeting me where I am, and allowing me the freedom to simply be me.

"Through Personal Branding You Control How Others See You."

– Yolanda M. Smith

Introduction

As someone who spent decades in the world of marketing, sales, and professional relations, I can attest to the power of a strong brand, and especially a powerful personal brand. Whether you're an entrepreneur, influencer, corporate professional or simply seeking to establish yourself as an authority in your field, a well-crafted personal brand can be the key to success.

To help you on this journey, I've compiled seven strategies for scaling your personal brand. These strategies will guide you in defining your unique value proposition, understanding and attracting your audience, being consistent in your messaging and behavior, telling your story, building your network, continuously learning, and most importantly, being authentic.

By implementing these strategies, you can build a personal brand that stands out, and ultimately helps you achieve visibility, recognition and success. So, without further ado, let's dive in and discover how to get your brand maximum impact.

"Branding is the Art of Becoming Knowable, Likable and Trustable."

– John Jantsch

Chapter 1

Focus On Your Unique
Value Proposition (UVP)

To succeed in building a strong personal brand, you must know what sets you apart from others. Define your UVP and use it to create a unique brand that stands out in your industry. In today's world, a personal brand is a requirement and not an option.

A Unique Value Proposition (UVP), also known as a Unique Selling Proposition (USP), is a statement that summarizes the unique benefit or advantage that a product, service, or brand provides to its customers or target audience. It's a clear and concise statement that communicates why someone should choose you product or service over your competitors'.

In the context of personal branding, your UVP refers to the unique value that you offer to your audience or potential clients. It's what sets you apart from others in your field or industry and makes you stand out. Your UVP should communicate the unique skills, experiences, and qualities that you possess and how they benefit your audience. By establishing a clear and compelling UVP, you can differentiate yourself and attract the right audience to your personal brand.

Your UVP should answer the question, "Why should someone choose your brand over others?" It's a powerful tool that helps you stand out in a crowded market and attract customers who resonate with your brand's values and personality.

To develop your UVP, consider the following questions:

- What is your superpower and expertise?

  _____

  _____

  _____

  _____

  _____

- What are the key benefits of your product or service?

  _____

  _____

  _____

  _____

  _____

- What makes your product or service different from others in the market?

  _____

  _____

  _____

  _____

  _____

- What problems or pain points does your product or service solve for your target audience?

  _____

  _____

  _____

  _____

  _____

- What unique qualities or characteristics do you bring to the table?

  _____

  _____

  _____

  _____

  _____

- What is your brand's mission or purpose?

_____

_____

_____

_____

_____

Use the answers to these questions to craft a clear and concise UVP that communicates your value proposition to your target audience. Your UVP should be memorable, easy to understand, and should differentiate you from your competitors in a meaningful way. Once you have a strong UVP, you can use it to guide all aspects of your personal brand, from your messaging and content to your visual identity and marketing strategies.

UNIQUE VALUE PROPOSTION STATEMENT:

_____

_____

_____

_____

_____

_____

_____

_____

_____

_____

_____

_____

_____

"*When you speak to everyone,*
you speak to no one."

– Meredith Hill

Chapter 2

Know Your Audience

Understanding your audience is key to building a strong personal brand. Who are your ideal clients or customers? What do they need? What do they want? What problems are they trying to solve?

Use this information to create content and marketing strategies that resonate with your audience and help you connect with them on a deeper level. Knowing your audience is crucial to building a strong personal brand because it helps you understand who you're creating content for and what they need and want from you. When you know your audience, you can tailor your messaging, content, and marketing strategies to resonate with them on a deeper level.

Here are a few reasons why knowing your audience is so important:

1. It helps you create content that resonates with your audience: When you know who your audience is and what they care about,

you can create content that speaks to their needs and interests. This helps you build a deeper connection with your audience and increases the likelihood that they'll engage with your content and share it with others.

2. It helps you build trust: When your audience feels that you understand them and their needs, they're more likely to trust you and view you as an authority in your industry. This can lead to increased loyalty and long-term relationships with your audience.

3. It helps you make informed business decisions: When you know who your audience is, you can use this information to make informed decisions about your business. For example, you can use audience data to determine which products or services to offer, which marketing channels to focus on, and how to price your offerings.

4. It helps you stand out in a crowded market: When you know your audience and what they need and want, you can differentiate yourself from your competitors by offering unique solutions to their problems or by addressing their pain points in a way that no one else is.

In summary, knowing your audience is essential to building a strong personal brand. By understanding who your audience is and what they need and want, you can create content that resonates with them, build trust, make informed business decisions, and stand out in a crowded market.

"

"Consistency is the DNA of Mastery."

– Robin S. Sharma

Chapter 3

Be Consistent

Consistency is key to building a strong personal brand. Whether it's your messaging, your visual identity, or your content, make sure that everything you do reflects your brand's values and personality. Being consistent is an essential aspect of building a strong personal brand. Consistency means that your messaging, visual identity, and overall brand personality are aligned across all touchpoints, including your website, social media channels, email communications, and any other platform where you interact with your audience.

Here are a few reasons why consistency is so important:

a. It helps build trust: When your messaging and visual identity are consistent across all touchpoints, your audience knows what to expect from you. This consistency helps build trust and credibility with your audience.

b. It reinforces your brand's personality and values: Consistency in messaging and the overall look and feel strengthens your brand's personality and values, making it easier for your audience to understand who you are and what you stand for.

c. It makes your brand more memorable: Consistency also helps your brand stand out in a crowded market and makes it more memorable for your audience. You definitely want to be memorable, for all the right reasons.

d. It creates a cohesive brand experience: Consistency creates a cohesive brand experience for your audience, no matter where they interact with you. This helps create a sense of continuity and familiarity that can lead to increased engagement and loyalty.

To maintain consistency in your personal brand, start by defining your brand's messaging and visual identity. Your messaging should include your UVP, brand personality, authenticity and tone of voice. Your visual identity should include your logo, color scheme, typography, and other design elements.

Once you have defined your messaging and visual identity, use them consistently across all touchpoints. This includes your website, social media channels, email communications, and any other platform where you interact with your audience. By maintaining consistency, you'll build trust, be discoverable, reinforce your brand's personality and values, make your brand more memorable, and create a cohesive brand experience for your audience.

Remember, if you are not consistent with your brand online and offline, you run the risk of creating brand confusion. And one thing for certain is that confused people do not buy. Period!

"If Relationships are the New Currency,
Storytelling is the Connection."

– Yolanda M. Smith

Chapter 4

Embrace Storytelling

I believe in the power of storytelling to connect with an audience. Use stories to convey your brand's message and values, and to engage your audience on an emotional level. Storytelling is an essential component of building a strong personal brand because it helps you create a deeper emotional connection with your audience. When you tell a compelling story, you can convey your brand's values, mission, and personality in a way that resonates with your audience on a deeper level.

Here are a few reasons why storytelling is so important:

a. It helps your audience connect with your brand on an emotional level: When you tell a story, you create an emotional connection with your audience. This connection can help build trust, increase engagement, and foster long-term relationships with your audience.

b. It helps differentiate your brand: When you tell a unique and compelling story, you can differentiate your brand from others in your industry. This can help you stand out in a crowded market and make your brand more memorable.

c. It helps convey your brand's values and personality: A well-crafted story can help you communicate your brand's values, personality, and mission in a way that resonates with your audience. This can help you build a deeper connection with your audience and increase brand loyalty.

d. It helps make complex ideas more accessible: Stories can help you make complex ideas more accessible to your audience. By using a narrative structure, you can help your audience understand abstract concepts and ideas in a way that is easier to digest.

To incorporate storytelling into your personal brand, start by identifying the key messages you want to convey to your audience. Then, think about how you can use storytelling techniques to communicate those messages in a way that connects with your audience.

Consider using a narrative structure, such as the hero's journey or problem solution to build your story. The hero's journey is a common narrative story template, that involves a hero who goes on an adventure, learns a lesson, wins a victory with that newfound knowledge, and then returns home transformed. The hero's journey can be boiled down to three essential stages:

- **The departure**. The hero leaves the familiar world behind.
- **The initiation**. The hero learns to navigate the unfamiliar world.
- **The return**. The hero returns to the familiar world.

The Problem→Solution approach is a great technique, that will help you his is a classic story structure that divides the story into three acts: the setup, confrontation, and resolution. The first act establishes the setting, characters, and conflict. The second act involves the character facing various obstacles and challenges in their attempt to overcome the conflict. The third act is the resolution, where the conflict is resolved, and loose ends are tied up. The key to storytelling is to tell the story from your heart using vivid imagery and sensory details to help your audience visualize your story. Bring them to that moment in time with you, and make sure your story is authentic and true to your brand's values and personality.

By incorporating storytelling into your personal brand, you can create a deeper emotional connection with your audience, differentiate your brand, convey your brand's values and personality, and make complex ideas more accessible to your audience.

"Your network is your net worth."

– Porter Gale

Chapter 5

Build Your Network

Your personal brand is only as strong as your network. You've likely heard the saying; connection is the new currency. Build relationships with others in your industry, collaborate with other professionals, influencers and entrepreneurs, and engage with your audience to expand your reach. Building a network is an essential aspect of building a strong personal brand. A strong network can help you connect with potential clients, partners, mentors, and other professionals in your industry. It allows you to increase your influence and build authority for your expertise and superpowers.

Here are a few strategies for building your network:

    a. Attend industry events: Attending industry events is a great way to meet new people and connect with other professionals in your industry. Look for conferences, trade shows, and other events that are relevant to your field and make an effort to attend them.

b. Join professional organizations: Joining professional organizations can help you meet other professionals in your industry and stay up to date on industry trends and best practices. Look for organizations that align with your interests and goals and become an active member. For example, if you are a woman business owner, the National Association of Women Business Owners is a national organization that can increase your network and access to other business owners. Another great association is the Chamber of Commerce or the Small Business Association in your area.

c. Participate in online communities: There are many online communities, such as LinkedIn and Facebook groups and industry-specific forums, where you can connect with others in your field. Participate in these communities by sharing your expertise, asking questions, and engaging in discussions.

d. Reach out to people directly: If there is someone you admire or would like to connect with, don't be afraid to reach out to them directly. Send them an email or a message on social media introducing yourself and expressing your interest in connecting with them.

e. Attend networking events: Networking events, such as happy hours, breakfast meetings, local or industry-specific events, are a great way to meet new people and expand your network.

f. Build a powerful social network through social media. Social media is a great tool that allows you to communicate, engage, inform, and empower others. Don't be a passive spectator, instead follow influencers and the competition in your industry of field of expertise, along with people you wish to connect with and be sure to like, share, and comment on their posts and content.

When building your network, it's important to focus on quality over quantity. Instead of trying to connect with as many people as possible, focus on building meaningful relationships with a select group of individuals who can help you achieve your goals. Make sure you are clear about your goals and what you have to offer. Be proactive in reaching out to others and offering your expertise and support. Adding value and serving others is more rewarding personally and financially.

And don't forget to maintain and nurture your relationships by staying in touch and following up regularly. Building a strong network allows you to create opportunities for yourself and your personal brand and increase your visibility in your industry.

"Be Yourself, Everyone Else Is Already Taken."

– Oscar Wilde

Chapter 6

Be Authentic

Your personal brand should be an authentic reflection of who you are and what you stand for. Don't try to be someone you're not or pretend to have values that don't align with your true self. People can sense when someone is being inauthentic, and it can damage your brand in the long run. Authenticity is a critical aspect of building a strong personal brand. Authenticity means being true to yourself and your values and communicating those values to your audience in a way that is genuine and sincere. When your personal brand is authentic, your audience can trust you and connect with you on a deeper level.

Here are a few ways to evaluate your authenticity:

a. Consistency: We have talked about this as it relates to your brand. Authenticity requires consistency in both your words and your actions. Make sure your brand messaging aligns with your behavior and that you are consistently living up to your brand values.

b. Transparency: Authenticity requires transparency and honesty. Be open and honest with your audience about your goals, challenges, and successes.

c. Vulnerability: Authenticity also requires vulnerability. Share your personal stories and experiences with your audience to show that you are human and relatable.

d. Receptiveness: Authenticity requires receptiveness to feedback and criticism. Be willing to listen to your audience and make changes to your brand as necessary.

e. Originality: Authenticity requires originality. Don't copy other brands or try to be something you're not. Instead, focus on what makes you unique and communicate that to your audience. You're an original, why be a copy?

To evaluate your authenticity, start by reviewing your brand messaging and values. Are they consistent with your behavior and actions? Are you being transparent and honest with your audience? Are you willing to be vulnerable and receptive to feedback? And are you communicating what makes you unique and original?

It can also be helpful to ask for feedback from others, such as friends, family, or colleagues. You want to ensure that the way you see yourself is how others see you as well. Ask them how they perceive your personal brand and whether they feel it is authentic. By evaluating your authenticity and making adjustments as necessary, you can build a personal brand that is genuine, trustworthy, and meaningful to your audience.

If you are interested in taking a validated brand assessment to see how others perceive you, contact me at info@branding4success.com.

Professionals and entrepreneurs worldwide are using the brand assessment tool to gain valuable insights to understand others perceptions of their personal brand so they can ensure how they view their brand is how others see it, and if not, take the necessary actions to develop a powerful personal brand. The assessment identifies your prominent attributes, strengths, brand personas, leadership skills and blind spots to help you create the brand you desire to position you for the results you deserve.

"Man's mind, once stretched by a new idea, never regains its original dimensions."

– Oliver Wendell Holmes

Chapter 7

Keep Learning

To be successful in building your personal brand, constantly learning and adapting to the changing landscape of your industry is a must. Stay up to date on the latest trends and techniques, and never stop learning and improving. You want to be viewed as the expert in your marketplace.

Knowledge is a crucial aspect of building a strong personal brand. Continuous learning helps you stay abreast of industry trends and best practices, and it can also help you develop new skills and expertise that can enhance your personal brand and offer a competitive advantage.

Here are a few tips to keep learning:

a. Read industry publications: Reading industry publications, such as blogs, magazines, and journals, can help you stay up to date on the latest trends and developments in your field.

b. Attend webinars and online courses: There are many online courses and webinars available that can help you develop new skills and expertise. Look for courses that are relevant to your field and interests.

c. Attend conferences and workshops: Attending conferences and workshops can provide you with valuable networking opportunities and exposure to new ideas and perspectives.

d. Seek out coaches and mentors: Coaches and mentors can provide valuable guidance and advice on how to navigate your industry and develop your personal brand. Look for coaches that have already done what you want to do and mentors who have experience and expertise in your field and who share your values and goals.

e. Experiment and take risks: Experimenting with new ideas and approaches can help you develop your creativity and innovation. Don't be afraid to take risks and try new things, even if they don't always work out.

f. Reflect and self-assess: Reflecting on your experiences and self-assessing your performance can help you identify areas for improvement and opportunities for growth. Take time to reflect on your successes and failures and use those experiences to inform your future actions.

By staying curious and committed to learning, you can continue to develop your personal brand and achieve your goals. Remember that learning is a lifelong process, and that there is always something new to discover and explore.

Conclusion

In summary, you are a brand, we are all brands. The question is, are you being strategic and intentional about your brand. You must be the CEO of your brand and take great diligence in building, mastering, and protecting your brand. Afterall, in the words of Warren Buffet, "it takes 20 years to build a reputation, and only seconds to tear it down."

Scaling your personal brand requires a combination of strategies and tactics. This is a journey, not a destination so give yourself grace and patience as you develop a powerful brand. Defining your Unique Selling Proposition (USP) is key to setting yourself apart from the competition, while understanding your audience is crucial for developing messaging and content that resonates with them. Consistency in your messaging, behavior, and brand identity establishes trust and credibility with your audience, and storytelling helps create a connection and differentiate yourself from your competitors. Building a strong network, keeping up with industry trends, and being authentic are also important components of scaling your personal brand.

By implementing these strategies, you can build a personal brand that stands out and resonates with your audience, and ultimately helps you achieve your goals. The benefits are endless and you have an opportunity to design your own destiny, whether it is helping others achieve, fulfilling your passion and purpose, growing your business, building generational wealth, developing a community, getting a promotion, gaining influence and authority or creating the freedom you desire to do the things you love with the people you care about. The bottom line is a personal brand is a powerful tool, and if you represent your brand confidently, appropriately, and consistently, the world can be your oyster. No dream, no destination, no goal is too big.

Connect with me to stay in the know on the latest branding strategies and tips:

www.yolandamsmith.com,

www.linkedin.com/in/branding4success

www.Instagram.com/Branding4success

Seven Questions

Seven questions to consider when scaling your personal brand.

1. Who is your target audience? Who do you want to reach with your brand?

_____

_____

_____

_____

_____

_____

_____

_____

_____

_____

_____

_____

2. What channels are you using to promote your brand? Are you utilizing social media, mail marketing, or other channels?

    _____

    _____

    _____

    _____

    _____

    _____

    _____

    _____

    _____

    _____

    _____

    _____

    _____

    _____

    _____

    _____

    _____

    _____

    _____

3. How consistent is your messaging across all platforms? Are you using a consistent tone, voice, and visual style?

_____

_____

_____

_____

_____

_____

_____

_____

_____

_____

_____

_____

_____

_____

_____

_____

_____

_____

4. What metrics are you using to track the success of your brand? Are you monitoring your follower count, engagement rate, or other metrics?

_____

_____

_____

_____

_____

_____

_____

_____

_____

_____

_____

_____

_____

_____

_____

_____

5. How are you engaging with your audience? Are you responding to comments and messages, and creating content that encourages interaction?

_____

_____

_____

_____

_____

_____

_____

_____

_____

_____

_____

_____

_____

_____

_____

_____

_____

6. Are you collaborating with other brands or influencers to expand your reach?

_____

_____

_____

_____

_____

_____

_____

_____

_____

_____

_____

_____

_____

_____

_____

_____

_____

_____

_____

7. What is your long-term vision for your personal brand? How do you see it evolving over time?

_____

_____

_____

_____

_____

_____

_____

_____

_____

_____

_____

_____

_____

_____

_____

_____

_____

NOTES

NOTES

NOTES

"Success loves speed."

– Spectacular Smith

90 Day Action Commitments to Scale Your Brand.

Spend some time reflecting on the seven strategies mentioned throughout the book and your answers to the above questions. Determine where you would like to experience improvement, or if you have yet to start in an area, now is a great time to get started. It is ok, remember we are on a journey, and it is an intentional journey. It is important to set goals because without them we have no destination and the journey becomes the road to nowhere. To be successful, we cannot aimlessly shoot in the dark, we need specific targets to realize our vision.

I am a big fan of the 12 Week Year. In the 12-Week Year, goal setting takes place every 90 days or every quarter. You are always in action, not waiting for the last quarter to achieve what we had all year to accomplish and did not. It reduces the desire for procrastination, complacency and most of all, you get things done. You will be amazed at how much you can accomplish using this technique.

When setting goals be sure to use the S.M.A.R.T. method. (Specific, Measurable, Actionable, Realistic, and Timely)

WEEK 1

WEEK 2

WEEK 3

_____

_____

_____

_____

_____

_____

_____

_____

_____

_____

_____

_____

_____

_____

_____

_____

_____

_____

WEEK 4

_____

_____

_____

_____

_____

_____

_____

_____

_____

_____

_____

_____

_____

_____

_____

_____

_____

_____

WEEK 5

WEEK 6

WEEK 7

WEEK 8

WEEK 9

WEEK 10

WEEK 11

WEEK 12

Programs and Services

- Keynote Speeches
    - Maximize Your Personal Brand
    - Personal Branding in the Digital Age
    - Branding the Authentic U

- Masterclass Facilitator
    - Creating & Maximizing your Personal Brand
    - Creating an Explosive Digital Footprint

- Corporate Teambuilding
    - Creating a Team Brand Identity

- Career Coaching
    - Group and Individual Sessions

- Online Course
    - Reputation to Reward: Creating and Maximizing Your Brand *Signature*

About the Author

Yolanda M. Smith

Yolanda M. Smith is a highly driven woman who was born to break barriers, she proves that when powered by purpose, people are unstoppable. Yolanda is an international speaker, author, and business strategist with expertise in personal branding and professional development. She's built her storied life and career brick by brick, fighting fears, failures, and setbacks to have the success she's always known was hers to claim. Her passion for empowering others to achieve their highest potential, led her to launch Branding 4 Success, LLC where she currently serves as CEO and Chief Brandthrupist™.

She is a certified brand analyst and coach who delivers keynote speeches and masterclasses on personal branding and professional development to academic, corporate, and professional organizations globally. Today she personifies what it means to ascend above adversity while inspiring countless others to do the same.

Connect with Yolanda at www.yolandamsmith.com, Instagram-@branding4success and www.linkedin.com/in/branding4success.

She inspires. She empowers. She unleashes.

Yolanda has extensive experience in healthcare where she held various leadership roles in the pharmaceutical industry. Known for her innovative thinking and ability to implement on her vision. Yolanda's recognition extends broadly. She received global recognition as the 2022 Brand Analyst of the Year and was named by the INC Magazine as one of "The Most Admired Women in Business 2022". Yolanda received recognition as a Top 10 Finalist in the 2020 Author Elite Awards for her book Reputation To Reward and was selected as one of the Indianapolis Business Journal's "Women of Influence," which recognizes women who have demonstrated professional excellence and leadership in their careers and community service to name a few.

Her educational pursuits earned her a Bachelor of Science degree from Indiana University, Kelley School of Business, in marketing and business analysis, and she obtained her MBA with a healthcare concentration from Indiana Wesleyan University. Yolanda holds an executive leadership certificate from Georgetown University. Yolanda is married with two children. She enjoys gardening and is a saltwater aquarium enthusiast.

More Books by Yolanda M. Smith

REPUTATION TO REWARD:

Mastering Your Brand Signature to Earn More, Lead More, Win More

MENTORING MOMENTS:

14 Remarkable Women Share Breakthroughs to Success

(Book & Journal)

Available at Yolandamsmith.com or through Amazon

www.ingramcontent.com/pod-product-compliance
Lightning Source LLC
Chambersburg PA
CBHW070505220526
45467CB00002B/586

* 9 7 9 8 3 9 0 7 2 0 8 9 9 *